The Cat with the Yellow Star

Coming of Age in Terezin

by Susan Goldman Rubin
with Ela Weissberger

Holiday House / New York

To the children of Terezin whose lives were
cut too short. Our memories of them live on.
— S. G. R. and E. W.

Text copyright © 2006 by Susan Goldman Rubin with Ela Weissberger
All Rights Reserved
Printed in the United States of America
www.holidayhouse.com
3 5 7 9 10 8 6 4

Library of Congress Cataloging-in-Publication Data
Rubin, Susan Goldman.
The cat with the yellow star : coming of age in Terezin / by Susan Goldman Rubin
with Ela Weissberger.— 1st ed.
p. cm.
ISBN 0-8234-1831-6 (hardcover)
1. Weissberger, Ela. 2. Jewish children in the Holocaust—Czech Republic—
Sudetenland—Biography—Juvenile literature. 3. Holocaust, Jewish (1939–1945)—
Czech Republic—Sudetenland—Personal narratives—Juvenile literature. 4. Jews—
Czech Republic—Sudetenland—Biography—Juvenile literature.
I. Weissberger, Ela. II. Title.
DS135.C97W45537 2006
940.53'18'083094371—dc22
2004057582

ISBN-13: 978-0-8234-1831-2 (hardcover)
ISBN-13: 978-0-8234-2154-1 (paperback)

title page: *Ela Weissberger
in June 1935 and an
example of the Jewish star
worn by all the Jews in
Nazi-occupied territories*

left: *Watercolor by
Ela Weissberger,
1943–1944*

PICTURE CREDITS
The following photographs and pictures from Ela Weissberger's personal collection
are reprinted by permission of Ela Weissberger: pages 1, 3, 4, 5, 6, 7 (all), 8 (all),
9 (right), 10 (above), 11, 12 (below), 13, 14 (all), 17, 18 (all), 19, 21 (right), 22, 25,
27, 29, 30 (all), 31 (all), 32, 33 (all), 34 (all), 35 (lower), and 36 (all).

The following works of art created by Ela Weissberger while she was interned in
Terezin and the photograph of the cast of *Brundibár* are used with permission from
the Jewish Museum in Prague: pages 2, 20 (all), 21 (left), 23, and 28.

The following photographs were taken by Ela Weissberger's cousin Walter Weiss in
1944 and 1945 and are now in the collection of the Simon Wiesenthal Center–Museum
of Tolerance collection: pages 12 (above), 15, and 16 (all).

The following pictures created by Helga Weissova while she was interned in Terezin,
"Arrival at Theresienstadt" (No. 3) and "Summons to Join the Transport" (No. 30),
are used by permission: Zeichne, was Du siehst: Zeichnungen eines Kindes aus
Theresienstadt/Terezin = Maluj, co vidis = Draw what you see, ed. by Niedersächsische
Verein zur Forderung von Theresienstadt/Terezin e. V., No. 3 and 30 © Wallstein
Verlag Göttingen, 1998: pages 10 (below) and 26.

The Jewish star on pages 1 and 9 is reprinted courtesy of the Simon Wiesenthal
Center Library and Archives, Los Angeles, California.

The music from the children's opera *Brundibár* on page 24 is used with permission:
© Copyright 1993 by Tempo Praha, a Boosey & Hawkes company. Reprinted by
permission of Boosey & Hawkes, Inc.

The top photograph on page 35 is used with permission of the Los Angeles Opera,
Madison Project of Santa Monica College. Photographer, Randy Bellous.

Contents

Ela, right; her sister, Ilona, left; and their nanny, Marie Franková, vacationing at Karlovy Vary, which is now in the Czech Republic, 1934

A group that includes Ela's relatives and family friends taking a tour of the famous sandstone formations in the Cesky Raj region of what is now the Czech Republic. Ela's father, Max Stein, is the second from the right. Ela's mother, Marketa Stein, is second from the left. Ela is third from the right under the arm of her school's principal. Ela's sister, Ilona, is the girl peeking out from above, 1936.

Chapter 1
Sudetenland,
November 1938:
Kristallnacht

Jews Out!

Ela Stein, eight years old, stared in horror at the words painted on her front door. Her heart thumped with fear. Broken glass lay everywhere. She clutched her big sister Ilona's hand. Last night they had heard townspeople marching toward their house. Beating drums. Shouting. Smashing windows downstairs. She and Ilona and their mother and aunt who was staying with them had run upstairs to the attic and had huddled together for hours to keep warm and safe until it was all over.

Now their mother hurried them back into the house and told them to keep the door locked. She had been ordered to report to Nazi headquarters.

In October Nazi troops had invaded a part of Czechoslovakia where Ela lived called Sudetenland and had annexed it to Germany. In Ela's town, Lom u Mostu, they had taken over the school next door. One day at the German barbershop, where Ela's father had gone to hear the news, he dared to speak out against Adolf Hitler, leader of the Nazi Party. That very night police and townspeople had come to Ela's house and had taken her father away. Ela had not seen him again and didn't know where he was. He had simply disappeared.

Ela's father, Max Stein, celebrates his birthday with his family in January 1927. Max Stein is seated second from the left, playing an accordion. The baby next to him is Ela's sister, Ilona. Ela's mother, Marketa Stein, is holding Ilona.

Ela was born in this house belonging to her grandparents in the village of Lom u Mostu, now in the Czech Republic. She lived there with her family until November 1938.

When Ela's mother came back from Nazi headquarters, she told Ela they would have to leave immediately. There was no time to pack anything. Ela's Uncle Vojta waited outside on his motorcycle, and they jumped on. "It was cold for Ilona and me in the sidecar," Ela remembered. Cold rain mixed with snow stung her face as they sped along. At the border between Sudetenland and what was left of Czechoslovakia, a Nazi officer stopped them.

Ela burst into tears. "Mommy, I want to go home."

Perhaps her tears softened the officer's heart. He looked at Ela. Then he yelled, "*Schnell!* Now, run!" They leaped off the motorcycle and dashed across the border into Czechoslovakia.

Chapter 2
Prague, Czechoslovakia
1938–1942

Dr. Otto Altenstein, Ela's Uncle Otto, 1936

"Surely we'll be safe here in this beautiful city," thought Ela. She loved the winding streets, the towering cathedrals with bells chiming, the castle high on a hill like a picture in her fairy-tale book.

At first they stayed with another uncle, Uncle Otto. Otto was Ela's mother's brother, and Ela adored him. "He was there for me, almost like my father," she said. But his apartment became too crowded. Ela's mother decided to send the girls to live with their grandmother in Brno. Ela and her sister went to elementary school there. "One day they took us out of school," remembered Ela. "Hitler came to town. They forced us to come out to greet him." The children lined both sides of the road. "He was in a car," said Ela. "He was standing and *heil*ing. We were afraid. I was scared to look at him." She remembered the night the Nazis had taken her father away because of what he had said about Hitler.

"I was so sick not to be with my mother," Ela said. So she and Ilona returned to Prague. "I came back when I was nine," said Ela. "My grandmother didn't want to stay alone in Brno. Later she came to Prague and lived with us."

Now that the Nazis were all over Prague, the city looked less beautiful. Troops had invaded in

Ela, her mother, and their cousins in Prague outside of Hradčany, the Castle District

Ilona and Ela, 1935

March 1939 and had taken over homes belonging to Jews. "They pushed us into a part of Prague where many Jews were living," said Ela. "We moved from place to place. Our last address was an apartment we shared with two other families. Again we moved in with my Uncle Otto."

Ela's last year at school was 1940. She treasured a class picture. The Nazis had passed a law forbid-

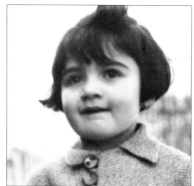

ding Jewish children to attend public schools. Jewish teachers taught the children in their homes, but it wasn't the same. Every day Ela watched longingly as her old friends walked by carrying book bags and soccer balls.

Now all Jews, even children, had to wear yellow stars printed with the word *Jude,* "Jew." "We had to be very careful," said Ela. "We couldn't be free."

Yet, despite everything, Ela liked to sing to herself as she walked along doing errands for her mother. One day a neighbor who belonged to the synagogue happened to overhear her. He noticed what a fine voice she had and invited her to sing at services every Friday night. Ela was thrilled!

Then in December 1941, the Nazis began rounding up Jews and deporting them. Some of Ela's friends were sent east to the Lodz Ghetto in Poland. Others went to a place called Terezin. One of Ela's aunts was sent there. In February

Ela's last year of school in Prague, 1940. She is seated in the front row, third from the left.

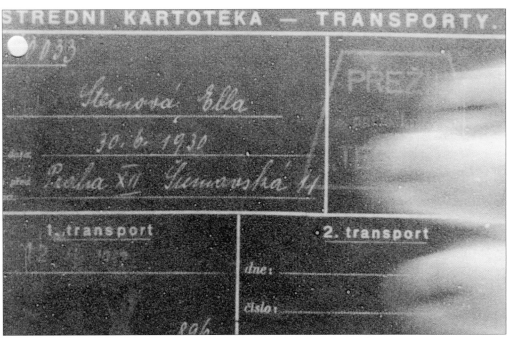

The Nazis ordered Ela, her family, and all Jews to wear a Star of David like this one.

Ela's registration card issued to her before she was transported to Terezin on February 12, 1942.

the Nazis ordered Ela and her mother, sister, grandmother, and Uncle Otto to go on the same transport. The word chilled them. *Transport* meant taking a train with other prisoners to the unknown. "We couldn't imagine how we would live there," said Ela. The Nazis gave them three days to get ready. They ran around the apartment wondering what to take. Ela's mother cut a big down comforter into three pieces, one for each of them, and had the edges stitched up to hold in the feathers. Every person was allowed to bring only 110 pounds of belongings.

The day they left Prague Ela's mother told the girls, "Wear as many dresses and sweaters as you can. They probably won't weigh us."

On February 12, 1942, Ela and her family boarded the train for Terezin. "I was eleven years old," she recalled.

Chapter 3
Terezin, Czechoslovakia, 1942–1943

The guard shouted for everyone to get off the train.

"We had to walk the last couple of miles in the snow," remembered Ela. "They put Uncle Otto at the head of the transport. He held on to me." Otto couldn't walk alone. As a child he had suffered from a bone sickness that had prevented him from growing from the waist down. Therefore, his legs were short for his body. Ela's suitcase

This photograph, taken in 1974, shows the railroad track inside Terezin. The building on the right is the Hamburger barrack where Ela lived with her mother and sister until June 1942, when she moved to the children's barrack.

Arrival in Terezin *by Helga Weissova*

A photograph of Terezin taken in 1974

got heavier and heavier as she dragged it along while helping her uncle.

"March! March!" screamed ghetto guards carrying billy clubs. Ela's mother whispered that Terezin (Theresienstadt in German) had been an army fortress before the Nazis turned it into a ghetto for Jews. Now the SS, Adolf Hitler's special squads, ran the camp. Nazi officers armed with rifles and wearing swastika armbands kept watch as Ela and her mother, sister, uncle, grandmother, and a thousand other new prisoners marched through huge wooden gates that clanged shut behind them. "When the door closed, we knew we were locked up," said Ela.

"They separated us. My grandmother went to another barrack." Uncle Otto was sent to a barrack for men. At first Ela stayed in a tiny, crowded room in a barrack with her mother and sister. "It was horrible," said Ela. "So cold."

Around her, people lay sick and dying from disease and hunger. There wasn't enough to eat, and what there was tasted revolting—watery green soup made from dried peas and bits of frozen potatoes. In the dirty courtyard Ela saw old men and women searching through piles of garbage for rotten potato peels. They looked like walking skeletons. Many suffered from diarrhea. When Ela had to go to the bathroom, she stood in line

Karl Rahm was commandant of Terezin from February 1944 until May 1945. This picture was taken by Ela's cousin Walter Weiss during Rahm's 1945 trial in Litoměřice in what is now the Czech Republic. Ela's mother was a witness at the trial.

at the latrine, waiting her turn. The latrine smelled foul.

One night Ela went out to the corridor and heard the sound of prayers. Below in the courtyard she saw a rabbi holding a candle and saying *kaddish* over dead bodies. Thirty bodies were stacked up on a flat cart. Ela ran back to the room and huddled close to her mother, shutting her eyes tight. But she couldn't forget the corpses.

New prisoners kept arriving as the Nazis rounded up Jews from all over Europe. Thousands crammed into rooms and hallways. Some had to sleep on the stairs.

As Terezin became more and more overcrowded, prisoners, even children, were ordered to leave on transports to the East. No one knew what was there. Rumors spread that the Nazis had built a death camp in Poland, east of Terezin, called Auschwitz-Birkenau. Who would be sent next?

Ela's mother worked all day taking care of the Germans' garden. This was a relatively good job although prisoners were not allowed to take any vegetables.

"My mother was the best thief in Terezin," Ela said proudly. She once hid fifty tomatoes in her underclothes without squishing them because she had become so thin. "She didn't steal for herself," said Ela. "She exchanged vegetables for a little piece of bread or sugar so that we could have more. Many times she would give me a little package for those kids who didn't have parents."

Ela's sister, Ilona, moved into L410, a barrack for girls. By July Ela's mother told Ela that she wanted her to stay there too because it would be

Special ghetto money was printed in Terezin.

12

better for her. The Jewish Council of Elders, a group of Jews ordered to govern the camp under Nazi rule, had set up "homes" for the children. Caretakers, who were also prisoners, looked after the children while their parents worked. The Council gave the children a little more food and a slightly better place to live.

Ela didn't want to leave her mother. The homes' educational staff allowed the children to visit their parents and relatives for only an hour every other day. Sometimes not at all. The rules kept changing. But reluctantly Ela agreed to go and packed her suitcase. "We knew it would be better," she said.

A ghetto post office was opened on November 24, 1942, in Terezin. This postcard is stamped on the opening day.

Chapter 4
Terezin, 1942–1943

Ella Pollak, called Tella, one of the caretakers in Room 28

In Room 28 lived about twenty-eight girls, all Ela's age. Ela wondered if they would be her friends. The only girl she knew was Eva Winkler, who had also been in the barrack.

The caretakers, Eva and Tella, assigned the girls to places in the triple-decker bunks that filled the room. Ela shyly admitted that she walked in her sleep, so they let her have a bottom bunk. Right away she became good friends with the girls beside her: Anna Flach, nicknamed Flaska because her last name meant "bottle" in Czech, and Ruth Schachter, called Bunny because her large front teeth looked like a rabbit's.

Eva Winkler, with her brother, Jirka, in Switzerland, 1945

Being with other children took away some of Ela's misery. "We had each other," she said. "We loved each other."

The caretakers kept the girls busy. Tella was a piano teacher and gave music lessons. Since there was no piano, she taught Hebrew songs from memory. Tella explained that she was a Zionist, which meant that she hoped to live in the Jewish homeland, Palestine (Israel), someday.

At night, especially, Ela longed for her mother. The Nazis didn't allow prisoners to use electricity at night, and darkness made everything worse. "We tried to make the best of it," said Ela. "When it was dark, we used to sing and listen to stories, and so the time was passing."

One day Ela and a couple of the others helped Tella lug an old harmonium, a keyboard instrument like a little organ, up three flights of stairs from the cellar to their room. Now they had something like a piano for their lessons. "Tella

L410 is the building on the right side of the church. The window of Room 28 is the third from the left on the top floor.

wanted to play for us Smetana's *The Bartered Bride*," said Ela. "She was teaching us opera!" *The Bartered Bride* was the Czech national opera. Some of the best opera singers in Europe were prisoners who rehearsed down in the cellar after work. As a treat, Ela, Flaska, and Maria Mühlstein were allowed to go down and listen. Tella thought Ela had a particularly good voice and put her in the chorus of Room 28.

Flaska loved singing too. She and Ela and Maria were part of an organization called *Jad Tomehet* ("Helping Hand") in Hebrew. They visited the old people in their barracks and serenaded them. The girls called themselves the Allo Trio. "If it was someone's birthday, we went and sang a song," said Ela. "Or Tella would teach us a song in the person's language. If someone was ill, we tried as best we could to help. We would go to the train when some transports came and help old people carry their luggage. At that time the trains were coming inside the ghetto.

"I think we did a lot of good things," said Ela.

Old people at Terezin suffered the most. Ela's grandmother died of sickness in 1943. "There was no medicine to help her," said Ela.

From a scrap of blue cloth the girls of Room 28 made a flag symbolizing the spirit of the room. In the middle of the flag was a white circle, called a *Maagal* in Hebrew. "It was a circle, symbolizing perfection, and two hands tightly

clasped, for friendship," said Ela. *Maagal* became the name of the circle of friends.

"To become a member of the *Maagal* was a special honor," recalled Eva Winkler. "Tella strongly influenced us."

"She was strict, extremely strict," remembered Ela. "We learned discipline from Tella. We were like soldiers."

Tella's motto was, Clean mind, healthy body. She tried hard to keep the girls from catching

Ela's cousin Walter Weiss took these photographs of the camp from the church tower in Terezin. He was able to get up into the tower because it was his job to wind the clock there. His camera was smuggled into the camp by his Christian girlfriend. These photographs could not be developed until after Terezin was liberated in 1945.

typhoid like so many of the other children. Typhoid was an extremely contagious disease that killed many in the camp.

In those overcrowded rooms, rats, lice, and bedbugs spread disease. Tella believed that cold air killed bedbugs. Therefore she insisted on keeping windows open at night even in the middle of winter. "And we didn't have as many bedbugs as the other kids," remembered Ela. Not one girl in Room 28 came down with typhoid.

"Every morning we took turns airing out our bedding at the windows. Then she would take us to the [unheated] washrooms. We had to undress and wash up with ice-cold water."

The girls rotated chores. Sometimes Ela swept under the bunks, or went downstairs with a friend to get food rations for the whole group. "We would [each] get about an ounce of margarine, maybe a spoon of some kind of mar-garine, maybe a spoon of some kind of mar-malade, and a little piece of black bread," she remembered. "This had to last for three or four days. We used to mark on the bread how much we could cut out. Some kids were so hungry they finished the whole thing."

The girls ate on their bunks. Tella demanded that they use good manners.

"She wasn't liked by everyone," recalled Judith Schwartzbart. "It was no easy task keeping all of us girls reasonably peaceful under such terrible circumstances. No one knew what the Germans planned to do with us. The fear was always there. We were always terrified of new transports."

"'Invitations' to the transports mostly came in the middle of the night," said Ela. "They would wake us up. They would read to us from this little piece of paper who is chosen to go. This was very hard. They gave us four hours for the kids to be prepared."

This ghetto health record belonged to a relative of Ela's.

Ela and Her Friends from Terezin

Judith Schwartzbart, 1950

Handa Pollak, 1945

Eva Landa, 1938

Hanka Wertheimer, 1946

Helga Pollak, about age 10

Eva Winkler, 1945

Marta Frohlich, age 8

Marianne Deutsch, 1950

Eva Weiss-Gross, 1945 (caretaker)

Marianne Rosenzweig, 1943

Eva Eckstein, 1946 (caretaker)

Ela Stein, 1945

Anna Klein, 1945

Lenka Anna Lindt, 1941

The number of girls in Room 28 kept changing as some were sent away on transports and new girls arrived. Sometimes as many as thirty crowded in.

In January 1943, Helga Pollak moved into Room 28 and became one of Ela's best friends. The caretakers assigned her to a place beside Ela. Helga originally came from Vienna, but she had lived in Moravia and spoke Czech. Ela greatly admired her. Helga was smart, always writing in her diary, and a good student. She hoped to become a doctor someday.

In the morning the girls did schoolwork. Many Jewish prisoners at Terezin were university professors, scientists, actors, artists, and writers. They visited the children's rooms and secretly gave lessons. "Study in the ghetto was strictly forbidden by the Germans," recalled Eva Landa. "But we studied just the same!" One of the students stayed outside as a lookout and gave a signal if a ghetto guard or SS man came along. "I remember how afraid we were," said Hanka Wertheimer. "We knew that if we were caught, we would be punished."

There were punishments for all kinds of offenses. If anyone dared to pick a flower or a turnip in the field, he or she would be beaten. "Once three young boys ran away," wrote Helga Weissova, a girl Ela's age from Room 24 of L410. "For that we have already had a week of confinement to the barrack and no light." Another time, when Ela and her family had first arrived, they and the other prisoners were taken to the outer

Ela's sister, Ilona, sent this postcard from Terezin on February 28, 1942, to her Aunt Olga Kotek. Prisoners were allowed to write only thirty words in German. Ilona wrote that they had arrived safely and that they had found Rafi Schächter, a friend of the family, in Terezin.

walls and forced to view bodies of prisoners hanging from the gallows. Their offense was smuggling out letters.

Writing about Terezin and drawing scenes of daily life were forbidden. However, the girls made paintings, drawings, and collages recording their experiences and dreams. Friedl Dicker-Brandeis, a famous artist, came to Room 28 with art supplies. Tella's friends who were professional musicians instructed the girls too. "Her best friend, Gideon Klein, composed a song just for us," remembered Ela. "He would come to the room with Tella. They would sing the song and we'd repeat it."

In July 1943, Tella made an announcement. A children's opera called *Brundibár* was going to

Ela created these drawings and painting in classes with Friedl Dicker-Brandeis from 1943–1944

This watercolor to the left is an illustration to a story Friedl read to the class. The students were only allowed to use the precious watercolors on rare occasions.

This pencil drawing is a portrait study.

This piece was done with brush and ink.

A portrait of Helga Pollak by Ela.

Rudi Freudenfeld smuggled the piano score of Brundibár *into Terezin.*

be performed at Terezin. Gideon Klein had asked her to select the girls with the very best voices to try out for parts. Ela was thrilled when Tella called her name along with Flaska, Maria, Bunny, and a few others.

"We went to the attic of the boys' home, L417, for casting," Ela remembered. The musical director, Rudi Freudenfeld, also called Baštík, and the conductor, Rafi Schächter, were there. Rafi had conducted the opera in Prague when it had first been performed at a children's orphanage. "They told us to sing scales," said Ela. Rudi struck a little tuning fork. "Our voices trembled with excitement," said Ela. "We were nervous about who would receive which role."

At last Rudi said, "Ela, you shall be the cat." She nearly jumped with joy. And from that moment on, whenever he saw her he whispered, "Kitty-Cat."

At the end of the day Ela went running to see her mother. "Ma, I will sing in an opera!" she shouted. "I'm the cat!"

Her mother looked puzzled. "What kind of opera has a cat?"

"Brundibár!"

Chapter 5
Terezin, 1943

Ela worried whether the Nazi officers would really let them put on an opera. Sometimes the guards seemed to look the other way and allowed prisoners to perform concerts and plays at the end of the day. Other times they forbade any cultural activities as a punishment.

Nevertheless, that summer Ela went to rehearsals of *Brundibár* a couple times a week in the hot, dusty attic of the boys' home. They started after Rudi had finished his work as a stonemason for the Nazis. "Sometimes he didn't have a chance to wash up," remembered Ela. "He didn't want to disappoint us." Rudi had smuggled in the piano score for *Brundibár* and played it on a small har-

In this postcard Ela's mother tells her sister-in-law, Olga Kotek, that Ela is singing in a children's opera that is bringing happiness to many people. All correspondence had to be written in German, so the guards could read it.

Meine Lieben,wir danken Euch und der 1.Erna für das Gesandte herzlich,denn es ist nach langer Zeit wieder eine Nachricht von Euch.Wir sind weiter recht gesund und guter Laune und freuten dasselbe von Fr.Epst ein über Euch gehört zu haben,Bitte,saget der 1.Erna unseren Dank und beste Grüsse.Die 1.Ela arbeitet auch schon in der Landwirtschaft.Sie trat in einer Kinderoper auf u.Ihr kö könnt Euch meine Freude darüber vorstellen.Für die einge löste Zulassungsmarke,danken wir bestens u.erwarten von Euch weitere Nachrichten.Auch der 1.Otto bekam ein Pa ket u.kommt ihm besonders das Fett sehr zu gute.Vielen Dank dafür,sowie für den ganzen Inhalt.Bleibet Alle rech gesund u.gedenket unserer,so wie wir Euerer gedenken. Post an uns könnt Ihr durch die Post schicken.Was macht Ihr immer?Warum schreibt Ihr uns nicht?Wir möchten so ge gerne wieder 'mal von Euch einige Zeilen lesen. Wir danken Euch u.allen Lieben nochmals für Alles u.ich schliesse mit den besten Grüssen und Küssen von Haus zu Haus u.bin Euere liebende
8.II.1!%%.

Grete

monium. The composer, Hans Krása, also a prisoner at Terezin, sat in on rehearsals. He and Rudi explained the story of the opera:

Little Joe and Annette, a brother and sister, need to buy milk for their sick mother. Out on the street they see an organ-grinder named Brundibár. When he plays a tune, people throw coins to him. Little Joe and Annette sing a simple song about ducks and geese, but adults don't like it and Brundibár chases the children away. That night Little Joe and Annette sleep beneath a wooden fence covered with posters. Animals in the posters—a dog, cat, and sparrow—come to life and offer to help Little Joe and Annette. In the morning the animals bring many neighborhood children to fight Brundibár. The animals attack Brundibár and he runs away. Then the animals and children sing a beautiful lullaby with Little Joe and Annette. This time people fill Little Joe's cap with coins, but Brundibár sneaks up and steals the cap. The children and animals chase him, catch him, and get back the money. The opera ends with a triumphant victory march.

"Honza, an orphan from Pilsen, got the role of Brundibár," said Ela. "Maria Mühlstein sometimes played Annette. Most of the girls in Room 28 sang in the children's chorus." Ela, like many of the others, did not know how to read music. "We learned by listening," she said.

In spite of choking heat, hunger, and constant fear of transports, they loved rehearsing. "Everybody knew everybody's role," said Ela. "When

The cast of Brundibár. *Ela, the cat, dressed in black is the fourth from the right in the front row. She stands next to Brundibár.*

we were singing, we forgot all our troubles. . . . It was possible to have hope."

The first performance took place on September 23, 1943, in the hall of the Magdeburg barrack, right under the Nazis' noses. The Nazis may have known about the opera but chose not to interfere.

František Zelenka, the original stage designer of *Brundibár* and also a prisoner at Terezin, had managed to re-create his scenery for opening night. Someone had found a piano without legs and propped it up on bricks. Gideon Klein

played. Other prisoners had sneaked in a little orchestra: guitar, clarinet, and trumpet. For a costume Ela wore her sister's black ski pants and her mother's black sweater. Zelenka painted whiskers on her face using tubes of makeup and a little box of shoe polish he had saved.

"When the people filed into the auditorium, we were all seized with stage fright," Ela recalled. "But when the first beat of the music sounded, we quickly got over it and forgot entirely where we were."

Words she spoke and sang as Cat expressed

her true feelings as a girl of Room 28:

> *"Let's extend our helping hand . . .*
> *Add your talent to our efforts,*
> *Voice to voice, and we'll be strong . . .*
> *United we'll win our stand."*

"As the opera drew to its close," said Ela, "and we sang the victory march, 'Brundibár Is Defeated,' there was—each time—thunderous applause."

Everyone at Terezin knew that Brundibár represented Hitler. Enthusiastically the whole audience joined in and sang,

> *"We've won a victory,*
> *Since we were not fearful,*
> *Since we were not tearful,*
> *Because we marched along*
> *Singing our happy song,*
> *Bright, joyful, and cheerful."*

"We were happy," said Ela, "and so was the audience. We all wanted to completely exhaust that moment of freedom. When we were onstage, it was the only time we were allowed to remove our yellow stars."

A sample of the score from Brundibár

Chapter 6
Terezin, 1943–1944

During that year Ela and the other children performed *Brundibár* every week. "We gave fifty-five performances," she recalled. "My mother came more than once." Ela hoped the opera could continue so that they could give fellow prisoners a little pleasure.

But transports of adults and children kept leaving for the East. As members of the cast were sent away on transports, they were replaced by other children. On May 18, 1944, Bunny Schachter, who sang in the chorus, was ordered to go.

Ela stayed on. Her mother still did gardening for a German officer. "This German told the commanders of Terezin that his workers would not be sent anywhere," remembered Ela. "At first my name was protected by my mother's name. Then I was listed for one or two transports, but my uncle somehow helped 'unlist me.'" Uncle Otto held an important position at Terezin as head of Social Programs and had some influence at that time.

In June 1944, Ela and the other leading characters performed the opera for members of the International Red Cross. The visitors had come to inspect conditions at the concentration camp. The Nazis wanted to trick them into thinking that Terezin was a "model camp" for Jews. So for the one-day visit, they beautified the camp and ordered the prisoners to put on entertainments

Ela created this crest from a scrap of wood she found. She burned out the illustration with a small magnifying glass. She gave the crest to her mother on Mother's Day in Terezin.

such as *Brundibár*. High-ranking Nazi officers in uniform attended the show. This time Ela and the children did the opera in a large auditorium in Sokol Hall. Prisoners who played in the orchestra used first-rate instruments that had been brought in especially for the occasion. The performance was a huge success. The Red Cross committee was completely fooled, so the Nazis decided to repeat the opera in August for a propaganda film titled *Hitler Gives the Jews a Town*.

"The movie was almost the last performance," said Ela. "Kids weren't there anymore. There were so many transports. Eva Landa had been the first to go in December 1943. Gideon Klein and all the musicians left."

In September and October the number of transports rose sharply. One by one Ela's friends in Room 28 were summoned to go: Hanka Wertheimer, Judith Schwartzbart, Lenka Lindt. . . .

Eva Fischl, Hanna Lissau, and Maria Mühlstein went on the same day, October 16, 1944. Even Tella was forced to leave.

On the night of October 22, Helga Pollak received a slip of paper ordering her to go on a transport. Early the next morning Ela went to the train to say good-bye. SS officers stood guard as the cattle cars were loaded with prisoners. Ela wondered if she would ever see her dear friend Helga again.

Now there were only three girls left in Room 28 beside Ela. They tore their blue-and-white *Maagal* flag into four pieces. Each girl took a piece and promised to put the flag back together after the war.

Summons to Join the Transport *by Helga Weissova*

Chapter 7
Terezin, 1944–1945

Ela lost her piece of the flag, but she did not give up hope.

"Room 28 became like a ghost town when all the children were taken away," she said. "I moved with my mother and sister to a room in a house near the fields of Terezin."

Ela's Uncle Otto was sent away on the last transport, October 28, 1944. "I really wanted to go with him," she recalled. "I sneaked into that place where they [the prisoners] stayed [before getting into the cattle cars]. The Nazis didn't let me through."

Now Ela worked in a garden with a group of other young people. Her sister gardened in a different spot with adults. Sometimes Ela saw an American plane flying overhead and waved. Would the war end soon? Would her friends reunite and form the *Maagal* once more?

In the late afternoon of a day in March or

Ela created this chalk drawing while in Terezin. The darker lines are corrections made by Friedl Dicker-Brandeis.

April 1945, Ela was standing outside on the deck of her house near the opening of the ghetto. Someone yelled, "The women are coming!"

"Hundreds of people streamed back into Terezin," said Ela. "I couldn't recognize anyone." Word quickly spread that the prisoners had been on a Death March. The Nazis knew they were losing the war as Allied troops approached. So they emptied the death camps "in the East" that had been established for the mass killing of Jews and forced prisoners to march toward Germany. Thousands died along the way. But some made it back to Terezin.

"They were skeletons, dragging along, in terrible condition," remembered Ela. "It was still very cold. Some came in stockings all torn.

"I kept looking and looking, and all of a sudden I saw my friend Helga, and I started to yell, 'Helga! Helga!' I was screaming, 'Helga is here! Helga is here!' I wanted to welcome her before she was taken to quarantine where they were being led because they were all ill. And that's how I found my Helga again."

Later, as Helga recovered, she told Ela about the Auschwitz-Birkenau Extermination Camp, where she had been sent. It was a miracle, said Helga, that she had been selected to work instead of being gassed. This was the first time Ela and others knew what it really meant when people were sent "to the East."

On May 3, 1945, the Nazis turned Terezin over to the International Red Cross.

On May 5, Ela remembered, the first Russian tanks arrived on their way to Prague. "I will never forget," she said, "because it was my sister's birthday when the Russian army came in and freed us. I think this birthday was just for her. It was something fantastic! We couldn't imagine that we'd be free."

Ela created this collage while in Terezin. It is made from cut paper stuck down with flour and water, which was the only glue available.

Chapter 8
Czechoslovakia and Israel, 1945–1958

"Three and a half years I was at Terezin," said Ela. Upon liberation she was almost fifteen years old. Her sister, Ilona, was nineteen.

A few days later their Uncle Vojta came to look for them. He was the uncle who had taken them on his motorcycle across the border to Czechoslovakia. Uncle Vojta was not Jewish and therefore had not been imprisoned. He was not really their uncle either. His brother was married to Ela's Aunt Olga, one of her father's eight sis-

Vojta Kotek, Ela's uncle, picked up Ela and Ilona from Terezin on May 10, 1945.

ters. They still did not know what had happened to Ela's father, and they never found out. Uncle Vojta, a bachelor, deeply cared for Ela's mother and hoped to marry her, but she refused.

Ela's mother had to stay in Terezin for a while because a female Russian officer had chosen her to be a maid. Uncle Vojta took Ela and Ilona to his house in the town of Kolin. In her excitement Ela left most of her things behind. Ela's thoughts were on home. Her mother later sent some of Ela's things in a crate.

In Kolin, Ela eagerly started school and Ilona learned to be a dressmaker. By the end of the summer the girls moved back to Prague and found their own apartment in the same neighborhood where they had lived before. Soon their mother joined them. One day, on the stairs of her building, Ela bumped into her friend Flaska. "We couldn't believe it!" said Ela. It turned out that Flaska was visiting her older brother, who lived in the same building. She gave Ela her address in Brno, and the girls exchanged letters. Ela was attending art school, and Flaska was studying at the music conservatory. Ela also stayed in touch with two other girls from Room 28 who lived in Prague.

On May 6, 1946, everyone in Prague celebrated the first anniversary of the end of the war. Ela joined crowds dancing in Wenceslas Square. All of a sudden she heard someone whistling the victory march from *Brundibár*. It was Rudi Freudenfeld, the musical director! Ela was overjoyed to see him again. He still called her Kitty-Cat. He told her that any time he whistled a tune

Hanka Wertheimer, Handa Pollak, and Ela, in back, in Prague, 1947

Hanka Wertheimer and Ela in Prague after liberation, 1946

from *Brundibár* anyone who had been at Terezin would turn around and come over to him. Reminiscing, he said, "*Brundibár* was our life. We will never forget it."

Ela tried to find other friends from Room 28. However, many people, such as Rudi, had changed their last names to those that sounded less Jewish in order to get or keep jobs. Czechoslovakia was now governed by the Communist Party. Under this regime there was great anti-Semitism. Ela had often thought about going to Israel, the Jewish homeland. In 1949, she decided to move there, and her mother and sister went with her.

In Israel, Ela served in the army, and then the navy, and worked for the Secret Service. She met

Ela in spring 1947 when she was studying at the State School of Arts in Ceramics

Ela, right, and her friend Zahava, in Haifa, Israel, 1951

another soldier, Leopold Weissberger, who had been imprisoned at Mauthausen, a concentration camp in Austria. He had escaped by hiding underneath an empty freight car that usually carried charcoal. Ela and Leo fell in love and married. After their daughter, Tammy, was born, they decided to emigrate to America. Ilona had also married a man in Israel, and they too were moving to America. So their mother joined them and, in 1958, all started a new life.

Ela, a soldier in the Israeli navy in Eilat, Israel, 1951

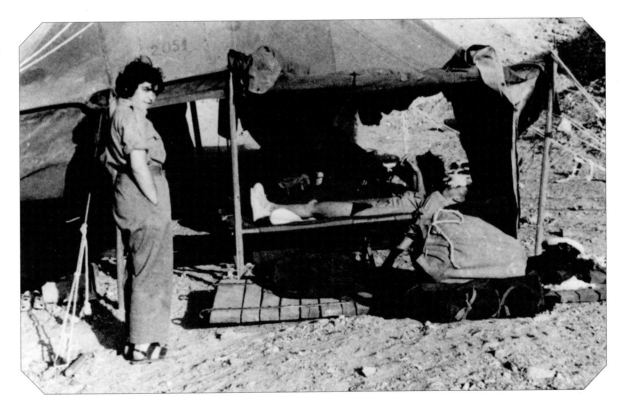

Chapter 9
New York, Vienna, and Prague, 1958–1986

In Brooklyn, New York, Ela kept busy taking care of Tammy and a second baby, David. She still thought about her friends in Room 28 and wondered if she would ever see them again. On a trip to Europe in the 1970s, Ela went to Vienna and Prague. She bought a book called *Terezin*, eyewitness memoirs, poems, and excerpts from children's diaries. "I came home, opened this book, and I was stunned," said Ela. There was an entry from the diary of her best friend, Helga Pollak. "She wrote about me!" Helga's married name was given and the city where she lived, Vienna.

Ela immediately wrote to a cousin in Vienna and said, "You must find my friend Helga."

"It took six months," she recalled. "Finally Helga and I started to write to each other. Nineteen eighty-six was the first time we met in person."

Ilona found out that there was going to be a gathering in Prague of the "Children of Terezin."

"I wanted to go," said Ela. "I called Helga and said, 'We will get together.'"

Helga came from Vienna. Flaska came from Brno. Eva Kohn lived in Prague. Eva Landa traveled all the way from Leningrad, Russia. And Marianne Deutsch came from Germany. "It was fantastic!" recalled Ela. "We were kissing, hugging, laughing, crying." They discovered that fifteen of the girls from Room 28 had survived.

Flaska still had her piece of the Room 28 flag. All the other pieces had been lost. Flaska gave her

A reunion of the girls from Room 28 in Weikersheim, Germany, 1999. From left to right are Judith Schwartzbart, Véra Nath, Helga Pollak, Anna Flach (Flaska), Marta Frohlich, Eva Landa, Eva Winkler, Hanka Wertheimer, Ela, and Handa Pollak.

quarter of the flag to Ela. Later, Ela stitched it to similar material to re-create the flag and sent it to Eva Winkler, who lived in Israel. Eva, the best at fancy needlework, embroidered the two clasped hands in the middle.

At the reunion they attended a performance of *Brundibár* put on by children from Radio Prague. At the end Ela and her friends joined in singing the victory march. Ela wiped away tears.

She and the girls promised to meet at least once a year. And they have kept their promise.

Ela, Anna Flach (Flaska), and Helga Pollak in Jerusalem, Israel, May 2000

Eva Stern and Hanka Wertheimer, in Israel

Anna Flach (Flaska), Eva Landa, Helga Pollak, and Ela

33

Chapter 10
Los Angeles,
California,
2003–2004

Ela with members of the Oswego Opera in Oswego, New York, 2001

After the 1986 reunion, Ela realized that she would probably never hear *Brundibár* again. "I thought the opera died," she said. To her amazement, though, around 1987 interest in the opera sprang up all over the world. Companies everywhere revived it. And every time it was performed, Ela was invited to attend.

On December 7, 2003, Ela sat in a darkened auditorium at the Simon Wiesenthal Center–Museum of Tolerance in Los Angeles, California. She applauded loudly for the children of the Los Angeles Opera who had just performed

Ela and Helga Weissova, at the far right, with the Zurich Young People's Theatre after a performance of Brundibár, *May 21, 1997*

Ela at Opera Camp 2004, a program of the Los Angeles Opera, Madison Project of Santa Monica College with the Simon Wiesenthal Center–Museum of Tolerance.

Brundibár and were taking their bows. Then Laura Stampler, who had played Ela's part, Cat, came down into the audience and got Ela. She led her onto the stage.

Ela faced the audience and said, "Sixty years ago we performed this opera at Terezin. Only a few of us survived. I lost many of my friends. But when we were performing *Brundibár,* we forgot where we were, we forgot all our troubles. Music was part of our resistance against the Nazis. Music, art, good teachers, and friends mean survival."

The conductor lifted his baton, and the musicians started to play the victory march again. This time Ela sang with the children. She sang in Czech and they sang in English.

"That day, when I heard it here in the United States sung by children who are free," she later said, "I knew it would never die."

Ela with Jessica Zemo, who played the cat in the Zurich Young People's Theatre production of Brundibár *in 1997.*

Author's Note

Almost all of the dialogue in this book was told to the author by Ela Weissberger in person or over the phone. Some came from a videotaped interview with Ela by the Survivors of the Shoah Visual History Foundation. Quotations from other people in Ela's life appeared in publications and were recorded in documentary films.

This is a true story.

Epilogue
So many went,
so few came back

10,632 children were sent to Terezin. 6,580 were sent "to the East": to the concentration and extermination camps in Poland where almost all were murdered. 322 were returned to Terezin. Only 4,096 children who had been imprisoned in Terezin survived. Of those, 15 lived in Ela's room.

top: *A collage Ela created at Terezin*

left: *A drawing Ela created at Terezin*

Today Ela speaks to many school groups. Here she is showing her yellow star.

ACKNOWLEDGMENTS

This book began when I was researching *Fireflies in the Dark: The Story of Friedl Dicker-Brandeis and the Children of Terezin*. I attended a performance of *Brundibár* put on by Opera Pacific in Irvine, California. In the parking-lot elevator I met Ela Weissberger. I immediately recognized Ela because I had seen and heard her in documentary films about Terezin. We became friends and exchanged phone calls. At a conference entitled "Art, Music and Education as Strategies for Survival" held at Moravian College, in Bethlehem, Pennsylvania, we started talking about collaborating on a book based on Ela's life experiences. Over the last few years we developed the idea as we visited each other's homes. We spent hours talking, and I taped a great number of our interviews. Together we looked through Ela's photos, and the pictures triggered more reminiscences. I thank Ela for entrusting me with her story and sharing her memories, precious photographs, and memorabilia. To me she is a true heroine.

I thank our editor, Mary Cash, for believing in this project and skillfully helping us shape Ela's story into a book. I also thank George Nicholson for developing the project with us and bringing to it his wisdom, warmth, and sincere dedication.

Many people generously assisted us with research. Alisah Schiller and Anita Tarsi, Director of Beit Terezin, Givat-Chaim Ichud, Israel, read our manuscript for accuracy. With the help of computers and a newly constructed database, they gave us updated information about the fate of prisoners at Ghetto Terezin.

My dear friend Adaire Klein, Director of the Library and Archives at the Simon Wiesenthal Center–Museum of Tolerance, made her library available to me as always. Fama Mor, former archivist at the Simon Wiesenthal Center–Museum of Tolerance, offered her help even after her retirement. I thank Adaire's entire staff and her team of volunteers for cheerfully working with me and providing me with necessary research materials.

My sincere thanks to the USC Shoah Foundation Institute for Visual History and Education for lending me videotaped testimonies to aid in my research.

And an enormous bouquet of thanks and appreciation to the Los Angeles Opera, Madison Project of Santa Monica College, for their collaborative productions of *Brundibár* with the Simon Wiesenthal Center–Museum of Tolerance. In particular I want to acknowledge Dale Franzen, Director, Special Projects, Madison Project, Santa Monica College; Stacy Brightman, Director of Education and Community Outreach, the Los Angeles Opera; Adam Philipson, Assistant Director, Madison Project and Opera Camp Coordinator, Santa Monica College; and Anthony Jones, Opera Camp Assistant Coordinator.

A huge thank-you to my group of writer friends for their weekly critiques and ongoing friendship.

Last but most definitely not least, I am grateful to my husband, Michael, for his loving and generous support.

S. G. R.

SOURCE NOTES

Each source note includes the first and last word or words of a quotation and its source. All book references are to publications cited in Resources (see page 38). For full information on Shoah interviews see page 39 under Interviews.

p. 5 *Jews Out!*: Ela Stein Weissberger, interview with author, May 5, 2000.

p. 6 "It was cold . . . home.": E.S.W., interview with author, May 21, 2004.

p. 6 "*Schnell!* Now, run!": E.S.W., videotaped Shoah interview, #2.

p. 7 "Surely we'll . . . father.": *Ibid.*

p. 7 "One day . . . look at him.": E.S.W., interview with author, May 21, 2004.

p. 7 "I was so sick . . . us.": *Ibid.*, May 22, 2004.

p. 8–9 "They pushed . . . there.": E.S.W., videotaped Shoah interview, #2.

p. 9 "Wear as many . . . us.": E.S.W., interview with author, May 5, 2000.

p. 9 "I was eleven years old.": *Ibid.*, January 6, 2000.

p. 10 "We had to walk . . . me.": E.S.W., videotaped Shoah interview, #2.

p. 11 "March! March! . . . cold.": E.S.W., interview with author, May 21, 2004.

p. 12 "My mother . . . parents.": E.S.W., videotaped Shoah interview, #4.

p. 13 "We knew . . . better.": *Ibid.*, #2.

p. 14 "We had . . . other.": *Ibid.*, #2.

p. 14–15 "We tried . . . things.": *Ibid.*, #3.

p. 15 "There was no . . . her.": E.S.W., interview with author, June 7, 2004.

p. 15–16 "It was a circle . . . friendship.": E.S.W., videotaped Shoah interview, #3.

p. 16 "To become . . . us.": Eva Winkler Zohar, in Dutlinger, p. 65.

p. 16 "She was . . . soldiers.": E.S.W., interview with author, January 10, 2003.

p. 17 "And we didn't . . . kids.": E.S.W., videotaped Shoah interview, #3.

p. 17 "Every morning we . . . water.": E.S.W., interview with author, May 5, 2000.

p. 17 "We would . . . whole thing.": E.S.W., videotaped Shoah interview, #4.

p. 17 "She wasn't . . . transports.": Judith Schwartzbart, in Dutlinger, p. 79.

p. 17 "'Invitations' . . . be prepared.": E.S.W., videotaped Shoah interview, #3.

p. 19 "Study in the ghetto . . . same!": Eva Landa, in Dutlinger, p. 66.

p. 19 "I remember . . . punished.": Hanka Wertheimer, in Dutlinger, p. 72.

p. 19 "Once three . . . light.": Helga Weissova, in *Terezin*, p. 105.

p. 19 "Her best friend . . . it.": E.S.W., interview with author, December 11, 2003.

p. 21 "We went . . . casting.": *Ibid.*, April 2, 2004.

p. 21 "They told us . . . role.": E.S.W., in Dutlinger, p. 68.

p. 21 "Ela, you shall . . . 'Kitty-Cat'": E.S.W., interview with author, April 2, 2004.

p. 21 "Ma . . . *Brundibár!*": *Ibid.*

p. 22 "Sometimes . . . disappoint us.": E.S.W., interview with author, December 3, 2003.

p. 22–23 "Honza . . . have hope.": *Ibid.*, December 6, 2003.

p. 23 "When the people . . . were.": E.S.W., in Dutlinger, p. 69.

p. 24 "*Let's extend . . . our stand.*": Hans Krása, *Brundibár*, libretto by Adolf Hoffmeister, first English translation by Joža Karas, Prague: Tempo Praha, 1993.

p. 24 "As the opera . . . applause.": E.S.W., in Dutlinger, p. 69.

p. 24 "*We've won . . . cheerful.*": Hans Krása, *Brundibár*, libretto by Adolf Hoffmeister, first English translation by Joža Karas, Prague: Tempo Praha, 1993.

p. 24 "We were . . . stars": E.S.W., in Dutlinger, p. 69.

p. 25 "We gave . . . once.": E.S.W., interview with author, December 11, 2003.

p. 25 "This German . . . 'unlist me.'": E.S.W., videotaped Shoah interview, #4.

p. 26–27 "The movie . . . Terezin.": E.S.W., interview with author, December 11, 2003.

p. 27–28 "I really . . . recognize anyone.": E.S.W., videotaped Shoah interview, #5.

p. 28 "They were skeletons . . . Helga again.": E.S.W., interview with author, May 5, 2000.

p. 28 "I will never . . . fantastic!": *Ibid.*, April 28, 2004.

p. 28–29 "We couldn't . . . Terezin.": E.S.W., videotaped Shoah interview, #6.

p. 29 "We couldn't believe it!": E.S.W., interview with author, May 21, 2004.

p. 30 "*Brundibár* . . . forget it.": *Ibid.*, December 10, 2003.

p. 32 "I came home . . . crying.": *Ibid.*, April 28, 2004.

p. 34 "I thought the opera died.": E.S.W., videotaped Shoah interview, #5.

p. 35 "Sixty years ago . . . survival.": E.S.W., closing remarks following production of *Brundibár* at the Simon Wiesenthal Center–Museum of Tolerance, Los Angeles, CA, December 7, 2003.

p. 35 "That day . . . die.": E.S.W., videotaped Shoah interview, #5.

RESOURCES

An asterisk (*) indicates works suitable for young readers.

Publications

Dutlinger, Anne D., ed. *Art, Music and Education as Strategies for Survival: Theresienstadt 1941–45.* New York: Herodias, 2001.

*Gilbert, Sir Martin. *Never Again.* New York: Universe Publishing / Rizzoli International Publications, Inc., 2000.

* Gutman, Israel, editor in chief. *Encyclopedia of the Holocaust.* Vol. 4. New York: Macmillan Publishing Co., 1990.

Huppert, Jehuda, and Hana Drori. *Theresienstadt: A Guide.* Prague: Vitalis, 2000.

Karas, Joža. *Music in Terezin 1941–1945.* New York: Beaufort Books Publishers in association with Pendragon Press, 1985.

*Rogasky, Barbara. *Smoke and Ashes: The Story of the Holocaust.* Rev. ed. New York: Holiday House, 2002.

*Rubin, Susan Goldman. *Fireflies in the Dark: The Story of Friedl Dicker-Brandeis and the Children of Terezin.* New York: Holiday House, 2000.

*Sendak, Maurice, and Tony Kushner. *Brundibar.* New York: Hyperion Books for Children, 2003.

*Sioras, Efstathia. *Czech Republic.* New York: Marshall Cavendish Corporation, 1999.

Terezin. Prague: The Council of Jewish Communities in the Czech Lands, 1965.

*Tylinek, Erich. *Prague: A Book of Photographs.* London: Spring Books, 1962.

*Weissova, Helga. *Draw What You See: A Child's Drawings from Theresienstadt.* Gottingen, Germany: Wallstein-Verlag, 1998.

Articles

Gates, Anita. "A Salute to Personal Acts of Resistance Against Evil." *New York Times*, September 10, 2004.

Kozinn, Allan. "In a Children's Opera, a Holocaust Connection." *New York Times*, February 13, 2003.

Midgette, Anne. "Sweet Tale for a Child, But a Dark Side, Too." *New York Times*, February 18, 2003.

Rubin, Daniel. "Art in the Midst of Hell." *Philadelphia Inquirer*, September 26, 2004.

Salamon, Julie. "Keeping Creativity Alive, Even in Hell." *New York Times*, September 10, 2004.

Thomas, Kevin. "A Tragic Command Performance." *Los Angeles Times*, February 26, 2004.

Waleson, Heidi. "An Opera That Survived the Holocaust." *Wall Street Journal*, February 6, 2003.

"What Friendship Means to You." *Newsday*, February 12, 2004.

Videos / DVDs

Clarke, Malcolm, and Stuart Sender. *Prisoner of Paradise*, DVD. Directed by Malcolm Clarke and Stuart Sender. Los Angeles: PBS, BBC u5 film production & History Television Canada, 2002.

* Hier, Rabbi Marvin, and Richard Trank. *Unlikely Heroes*, VHS. Directed by Richard Trank. Los Angeles: Moriah Films, 2004.

* Justman, Zuzana. *Voices of the Children*, A Terezin Foundation Inc. Production Videocassette. Written and directed by Zuzana Justman. New York: Cinema Guild, 1996.
* Krása, Hans. *Last Dance*, DVD. Directed by Mirra Bank. New York: First Run Features, 2002.
* Paul, Tamir. *Black & White Is Full of Colours*, VHS. Directed by Tamir Paul. Tel-Aviv, Israel: Argo Films and Czech TV in association with The New Foundation for Cinema and Television, 1996.

Weissberger, Ela. "Interview #38501, December 7, 1997." Interviewed by Kenneth Aran. 3 videos. Tappan, N.Y.: Survivors of the Shoah Visual History Foundation.
* Weissman, Dan, and Zuzana Justman. *Terezin Diary*, VHS. New York: First Run/Icarus Films, 1990.

Sound Recordings

* *Music From Terezin. Brundibár, A Children's Opera in Two Acts–Hebrew & Yiddish Folk Songs.* Vermont Symphony Orchestra. Robert De Cormier. With the Essex Children's Choir, members of the Vermont Symphony Orchestra & Chorus. Arabesque Recordings, Record ID# ARZ6680. ℗, 1996.

* *Brundibár, A Children's Opera in Two Acts–Czech Songs.* Composers from Thereseinstadt 1941–1945. Disman Radio Children's Ensemble. Joža Karas. Channel Classics Records B.V., Record ID# CCS5193. ℗, 1992.

* *Innocent Voices: The Verse of Terezin's Children.* Children's Choir, prepared by Barbara Orwick. John Federico. Lost Planet Records, Inc., FAN 0615548567825. ℗, 1996.

INTERVIEWS

Tarsi, Anita, Director of the Association Beit Terezin (Theresienstadt). Conversation with author, Woodland Hills, CA, October 29, 2004.

Weissberger, Ela. Closing remarks following production of *Brundibár* at the Simon Wiesenthal Center–Museum of Tolerance, Los Angeles, CA, December 7, 2003.

Weissberger, Ela. Telephone and in-person conversations with author: January 6, 2000; February 10–12, 2000; May 5–7, 2000; April 16, 2001; May 15, 2001; January 10, 2003; October 1, 2003; December 3, 2003; December 6–7, 2003; December 11–12, 2003; April 14, 2004; April 28, 2004; May 3, 2004; May 21, 2004; May 22, 2004; May 30, 2004; June 6–8, 2004; September 29, 2004; October 3, 2004; October 7, 2004; October 16, 2004; October 18, 2004; October 28, 2004; November 19, 2004; December 10, 2004; December 17, 2004; January 4, 2005; January 10, 2005; January 13, 2005; January 16, 2005.

INTERNET SITES

Jewish Museum in Prague
www.jewishmuseum.cz

Los Angeles Opera and Opera Camp
www.losangelesopera.com

Madison Campus Arts Project at Santa Monica College
www.smc.edu/madison/educational/educational_arts.html

Simon Wiesenthal Center
www.wiesenthal.com

Simon Wiesenthal Center–Museum of Tolerance
www.museumoftolerance.com

Survivors of the Shoah Visual History Foundation
www.vhf.org

Terezin Memorial (Pamatnik Terezin)
www.pamatnik-terezin.cz

Theresienstadt Martyrs Remembrance Association (Beit Theresienstadt)
www.bterezin.org.il/en_general_info.htm

United States Holocaust Memorial Museum
www.ushmm.org

Yad Vashem
www.yadvashem.org

INDEX

Page numbers in *italics* refer to illustrations.